Freaky Facts

hinkler

Published by Hinkler Books Pty Ltd
45–55 Fairchild Street
Heatherton VIC 3202 Australia
www.hinkler.com.au

hinkler

Cover illustrator: Rob Kiely
llustrator: Glen Singleton
Project editor: Katie Hewat
Designer: Diana Vlad

ISBN: 978 1 7418 2121 5

Printed and bound in China

Contents

Unusual Animal Facts

The giant squid has the largest eyes in the world.

A rat can survive longer without water than a camel.

The only bird that can fly backwards is the hummingbird.

A dolphin sleeps with one eye open.

A crocodile cannot stick its tongue out.

A mammal's blood is red, an insect's blood is yellow and a lobster's blood is blue.

Loud, fast music makes termites chew faster.

If termites have infested my furniture...and they love loud fast music...I'd better trade my HEAVY METAL collection for some slow quiet CLASSICAL MUSIC before they demolish the whole house!

A blue whale's tongue weighs more than an elephant.

An ostrich's eye is bigger than its brain.

Bats always exit a cave to the left.

Tigers have striped skin, not just striped fur.

Terry had to be careful in change rooms. For he had a secret. He was different from all the other tigers at school. Where they had stripes on their skin, Terry had spots!

The blue whale's whistle is the loudest noise made by an animal.

Camels have three eyelids to protect their eyes from blown sand.

A mole can dig a tunnel over 90 m (300 ft) long in just one night.

Elephants are not afraid of mice.

Elephants are not afraid of mice, but are very afraid of the similar looking Rogue Rwandan Rockhopping Rodent.

HI JUMBO!

Only female mosquitoes bite.

Snakes are immune to their own venom.

The fastest bird is the peregrine falcon. It can fly faster than 300 km (190 miles) per hour.

Mosquitoes are attracted to the colour blue more than any other colour.

Many species of reptiles have two penises.

Cats cannot taste sweet things.

Herons have been observed dropping insects on the water, then catching the fish that surface to eat the insects.

The largest egg is laid by the ostrich. An ostrich egg can be 20 cm (8 in) in length and 15 cm (6 in) in diameter.

11

The smallest egg is laid by the hummingbird. Its egg is less than 1 cm (0.39 in) in diameter.

Why you DON'T hear people saying... 'At breakfast...
I have my hummingbird egg... a piece of toast and jam
and a cup of tea and I'm off to work for the day!'

Bald eagles can swim.

A zebra is white with black stripes, not black with white stripes.

The bird-eating spider from South America can have a legspan of 30 cm (1 ft).

Statistically you are more likely to be attacked by a cow than a shark.

An eagle can kill and carry an animal as large as a small deer.

AHHRR, QUICK! Everyone out! There's a COW in the water!

At birth, a giant panda is smaller than a mouse.

To scare off enemies, the horned lizard squirts blood from its eyelids.

A blue whale's heart beats only nine times per minute.

A hedgehog's heart beats 300 times per minute.

Horses can sleep standing up.

When a baby kangaroo is born, it is about 2 cm (0.8 in) long.

An electric eel can produce a shock of 600 volts. That's enough to knock a horse off its feet.

Chimpanzees use tools more than any other animal, except humans.

Lobsters can regenerate their legs, claws and antennae if these parts are pulled off by a predator.

A bald eagle's nest can be 3.65 m (12 ft) deep and 3 m (10 ft) wide.

Parrots live longer than any other type of bird. There are reliable reports of parrots living to 150 years of age.

An African elephant has only four teeth.

Flying fish actually glide on wind currents. They can glide 6 m (20 ft) above the surface of the water.

Sea snakes are the most venomous snakes.

A scallop swims by quickly clapping its shell open and shut. This makes a water jet that pushes the scallop along.

Some captive octopuses have learned to open jars containing food. Many aquariums now give their octopuses puzzles and other games to keep them from getting bored.

Oscar, an octopus with plenty of time on his hands, contemplates an escape from the tank.

The lungfish can live out of water for as long as four years.

Polar bears have been known to swim 100 km (62 miles) without stopping.

Salamanders breathe through their skin.

A rhinoceros horn is made of compacted hair.

A woodpecker can peck up to 20 times per second.

Kiwi birds choose a mate for life. This can be up to 30 years.

Before seahorse eggs hatch, the male seahorse carries them in a pouch on his stomach.

A shark does not have bones. Its skeleton is made of cartilage.

Squirrels cannot remember where they have hidden half of their food.

The stegosaurus had a brain the size of a walnut.

It was always the Stegosauruses of the class that struggled in PHYSICS because of their walnut-sized brains.

An octopus has three hearts.

A penguin can drink saltwater because it has a gland in its throat that removes the salt from the water.

A giraffe has the same number of vertebrae in its neck as a mouse.

The Loch Ness monster is a protected animal under Scottish law.

A snail can sleep for three years.

An adult bear can run as fast as a horse.

Sheep can recognise other sheep from photographs.

Bees have five eyes.

Honeybees kill more people than venomous snakes.

Polar bears are left-handed.

Mosquito repellents do not repel. The repellent blocks a mosquito's sense of smell so it does not know a person is nearby.

A zebra foal can run with the herd an hour after its birth.

A polar bear's fur is not white, but translucent.

Some locusts have an adult lifespan of only a few weeks, after having lived in the ground as grubs for 15 years.

Butterflies taste with their feet.

Fleas that live on rats have probably killed more people than anything else because they spread bubonic plague.

The polar bear is the only mammal with hair on the soles of its feet.

American President John Quincy Adams owned a pet alligator. He kept it in the East Room of the White House.

Well Benedict my old friend. You're no longer the small alligator you once were. I fear you've outgrown my desk. I feel we need to set aside your own room at the White House.

Perhaps with its own lagoon... That would be nice.

Female ants do all the work.

A cockroach can live up to two weeks with its head cut off before it starves to death.

Dogs can make about ten vocal sounds. Cats can make more than 100 vocal sounds.

Walruses turn pink if they stay out in the sun too long.

There are 701 official breeds of dog.

Vultures have a unique defence mechanism; they throw up on their enemies.

A female pigeon cannot lay an egg unless she sees another pigeon. If another pigeon is not available, her own reflection in a mirror will do.

Cockroaches could survive a nuclear holocaust because radiation does not affect them as much as it affects other species.

The embryos of tiger sharks fight each other while in their mother's womb. Only the survivor is born.

Orang-utans protect their territory by burping loudly to warn off intruders.

Frogs can throw up. A frog throws up its stomach first, so that its stomach is dangling out of its mouth. The frog then uses its forearms to dig out the stomach's contents and swallows the stomach again.

Australian earthworms can grow up to 3 m (10 ft) in length.

There is enough poison in a poison-arrow frog to kill 2200 people.

A camel can drink up to 136 litres (30 gallons) of water at one time.

If a starfish is cut into pieces, each piece will become another starfish.

A dolphin can hear sound underwater from 24 km (15 miles) away.

A scallop has 35 eyes.

Some chimpanzees and orang-utans have been taught human sign language.

Most insects are deaf.

Before dolphins begin any group action, the pod holds a meeting. Each animal gets a chance to vocalise until a decision is made.

Snails produce a sticky discharge that forms a protective layer under them as they crawl. The discharge is so effective that a snail can crawl along the edge of a razor blade without cutting itself.

Earthworms have five hearts.

Some reptiles have eyes that operate
independently of each other, so that the
animal can see in two directions at once.

Groups of sea otters tie themselves together with kelp so they do not drift apart while they sleep.

A camel's hump stores fat, not water.

A daddy-long-legs spider is more venomous than a black widow spider but its fangs cannot penetrate human skin.

Bees are born fully grown.

Funny Phobias

Ablutophobia is the fear of bathing.

Who needs to have a bath... not me! There it is! That must be what I've got! ABLUTOPHOBIA ...a fear of bathing. Well...that's what I'll tell Mum anyway.

Alektorophobia is the fear of chickens.

Anablepophobia is the fear of looking up.

Arachibutyrophobia is the fear of peanut butter sticking to the roof of the mouth.

Basiphobia is the fear of walking.

Bibliophobia is the fear of books.

Chrometophobia is the fear of money.

Chronophobia is the fear of time.

Coulrophobia is the fear of clowns.

Genuphobia is the fear of knees.

Geumaphobia is the fear of taste.

Gnosiophobia is the fear of knowledge.

Gymnophobia is the fear of being naked.

Heliophobia is the fear of the sun.

Kleptophobia is the fear of stealing.

Lachanophobia is the fear of vegetables.

Logophobia is the fear of words.

Mnemophobia is the fear of memories.

Myrmecophobia is the fear of ants.

Nebulaphobia is the fear of fog.

Fearing a thick fog entering his loungeroom and engulfing him while sleeping infront of the TV... Harold closed all doors and windows...but failed to close Harry the cat's cat flap in the back door.

Ochophobia is the fear of vehicles.

A fear of vehicles drove Shirley to start a movement to bring back the HORSE for transport.

Due to his irrational fear of rain, Alex spent two days pinned to a wall under an awning waiting for the low pressure storm cell to leave his country.

Ombrophobia is the fear of rain.

Ornithophobia is the fear of birds.

Paraskavedekatriaphobia is the fear of Friday the 13th.

Peladophobia is the fear of bald people.

Philophobia is the fear of falling in love.

Esmerelda's fear of love was thinly disguised as a lack of interest.

Photophobia is the fear of light.

Pneumatophobia is the fear of air.

Pogonophobia is the fear of beards.

Somniphobia is the fear of sleep.

Syngenesophobia is the fear of relatives.

Tonsurophobia is the fear of haircuts.

Vestiphobia is the fear of clothing.

Wiccaphobia is the fear of witches and witchcraft.

Xenophobia is the fear of strangers or foreigners.

Zemmiphobia is the fear of the great mole rat.

Zoophobia is the fear of animals.

And finally . . .

Panophobia is the fear of everything.

George hid under his pillow when his fear of everything got to him...

Wacky World Records

The coldest temperature recorded on Earth was -89°C (-129°F) at Vostok, Antarctica, on 21 July 1983.

Charles Osborne had the hiccups for 69 years.

Bhutan was the last country to get the telephone. It did not have one until 1981.

The tallest tree in the world, a redwood, is 112 m (367 ft).

Just imagine a treehouse up there!

The biggest palace in the world is the Imperial Palace in Beijing. It has so many rooms that you could sleep in a different room every night for 25 years.

The largest iceberg was sighted in the South Pacific Ocean in 1956. It was 332 km (208 miles) long and 96 km (60 miles) wide, or about the size of Belgium.

Although covered with ice, Antarctica is the driest place on the planet with humidity lower than the Gobi Desert.

The longest time spent standing on one foot is 76 hours, 40 minutes.

The biggest pumpkin weighed 449 kg (990 lb).

The longest nose belonged to Thomas Wedders. It measured 19 cm (7.5 in). Thomas worked in a freak show in the 1770s.

The warmest temperature recorded on Earth was 57.8°C (136°F) at El Azizia, Libya, on 13 September 1922. Bath water is considered scalding at 46°C (125°F).

The largest crater on the moon is also the largest impact crater in the solar system. It measures 2100 km (1300 miles) across.

Strongman John Evans holds the world record for the heaviest weight balanced only on his head. He balanced 101 bricks that weighed 188 kg (416 lb).

The largest pearl ever found was the size of a tennis ball.

The pearl necklace is lovely dear... Though I am just a little concerned people may take it to be a tennis ball on a gold chain!

The fastest wind speed recorded was 508 km (318 miles) per hour in Oklahoma on 3 May 1999.

T.J. loses his best kite in 508 km winds... somewhere over Oklahoma in 1999.

Uhrrr... That was a good kite too!

The largest known volcano is Olympus Mons on Mars. It is 590 km (370 miles) wide and 24,000 m (79,000 ft) high. It is almost three times higher than Mount Everest.

The Holy See (State of the Vatican City) in Rome, Italy, is the smallest sovereign state in the world. It has a population of less than 1000 people.

The youngest graduate got his bachelor's degree in 1994 at the age of ten years, five months.

Dorothy Straight's first book, *How The World Began*, was published in 1964 when she was six years old, making her the youngest ever published author.

The loudest burp was 112 decibels (think jet aeroplane).

The record for holding one's breath underwater is 7.5 minutes.

The only time on record that snow has fallen in the Sahara Desert was on 18 February 1979. The storm lasted half an hour and the snow soon melted.

Abdul and his friend Ali didn't want to miss any of the brief half hour snow season over the Sahara Desert in 1979... so were ready to go.

Golf is the only sport that has been played on the moon.

The shortest war in history was fought between Zanzibar and England in 1896. The war had lasted for just 38 minutes when Zanzibar surrendered.

The longest recorded flight of a chicken is 13 seconds.

The world's smallest tree is the dwarf willow. It grows to 5 cm (2 in) on the tundra of Greenland.

The oldest known living thing is a bristlecone pine called Methuselah. It is located in the White Mountains on the California–Nevada border. The tree is estimated to be 4767 years old.

Hey Dad! Wait until you see what we've got! We've got us... A CHRISTMAS TREE!

Chucky brings home the 4767-year-old Bristlecone pine after a hiking trip to the White Mountains of USA.

The Guinness Book of Records holds the record for being the book most often stolen from public libraries.

Air hostess Vesna Vulovic of Yugoslavia fell 10,160 m (33,330 ft) from an aeroplane into a snowbound forest in Serbska Kamenice, Czechoslovakia, on 26 January 1972. It was the longest fall a person has survived.

It's Only Natural

An apple, potato and onion all taste sweet if you eat them with your nose plugged.

Watermelons are grown square in Japan so they take up less space and are easier to stack.

Jupiter is bigger than all the other planets in our solar system combined.

Hot water is heavier than cold water.

Natural gas has no smell. The smell is added for safety reasons.

Research indicates that plants grow better when they are stroked.

Strawberries contain more vitamin C than oranges.

Forty-one per cent of the moon is not visible from Earth at any time.

Pollen never deteriorates. It is one of the few natural substances that lasts indefinitely.

Because of the rotation of the Earth, an object can be thrown farther if it is thrown west.

Ninety per cent of all extinct species are birds.

The age of the universe is 13.7 billion years.

THE UNIVERSE TURNS 13.7 BILLION

Sound travels through water three times faster than through air.

True berries include the grape, tomato and eggplant, but not the raspberry or blackberry.

Pearls dissolve in vinegar.

The largest flower in the world is the corpse flower or *Rafflesia*. It grows up to 1.2 m (4 ft) wide and it stinks.

There are eight peas per pod on average.

In Calama, a town in the Atacama Desert of Chile, it has never rained.

Raindrops are not really shaped like drops; they are perfectly round.

In his quest to find out whether raindrops are perfectly round, Timothy stood in the rain for 24 hours ...not catching any raindrops... but catching a cold instead.

AAAAAHR

Lemons contain more sugar than strawberries.

When scientists drilled through the ice of Antarctica's Lake Vanda, they discovered that the water at the bottom of the lake was an amazingly warm 24°C (77°F). Ice crystals heat the water by focusing light onto the bottom of the lake.

The Amazon rainforest makes one-fifth of the world's oxygen.

The Antarctic ice sheet contains 71 per cent of the world's fresh water.

A tomato is a fruit, not a vegetable.

Lettuce is part of the sunflower family.

Water is the only substance on Earth that is lighter as a solid than as a liquid.

Coconuts kill more people than sharks do. Approximately 150 people are killed each year by coconuts.

AHHRR! EVERYBODY OUT! THERE ARE COCONUTS IN THE WATER!!

Remember the days when people would run screaming from the water because of us?

Yeah. Then someone worked out that coconuts killed more people than sharks?

The liquid inside young coconuts can be used as a substitute for blood plasma.

The only food that does not spoil is honey.

Fingernails grow nearly four times faster than toenails.

Hey! You're wasting your time chewing your toenails. Fingernails are better value! They grow four times as fast...and there's no smelly socks to contend with.

By raising your legs slowly and lying on your back, you cannot sink in quicksand.

It is impossible to sneeze with your eyes open.

Venus is the only planet that rotates clockwise.

Crunching Numbers

Buckingham Palace has more than 600 rooms.

I'm so sorry your Majesty! I didn't realise this was the bathroom!
There are just so many rooms in this palace!
Oh... and by the way Ma'am... There are still soap bubbles on your ladyship's nose!

The opposite sides of a dice always add up to seven.

Woodpecker scalps, porpoise teeth and giraffe tails have all been used as money.

A jiffy is an actual unit of time. It is one hundredth of a second.

Twenty per cent of all road accidents in Sweden involve a moose.

There are more than 200 lashes on a human eyelid. Each lash is shed every three to five months.

More than 1000 languages are spoken in Africa.

A porcupine has about 30,000 quills.

By the look of that little guy... I'd say I've got about 29,999 porcupine quills in my shorts! Give or take a few!

I wish people would look before they sit.

Humans have 639 muscles, but caterpillars have more than 4000.

Just twenty seconds' worth of fuel remained when Apollo 11's lunar module landed on the moon.

All it took was a twenty second dispute over where to land to turn the first landing on the moon into the first crash on the moon!

A solar day on Mercury, from sunrise to sunset, lasts about six Earth months.

There are more than 14,000 varieties of rice.

Cats can spend 16 hours a day sleeping.

After what amounted to sleeping most of the day, Harry the Persian slept most of the night catching up on the sleep he missed during the day.

A bee needs to flap its wings 250 times per second to remain in the air.

It takes 72 muscles to speak one word.

An alligator has 80 teeth.

It takes approximately 850 peanuts to make a standard jar of peanut butter.

The Great Wall of China is 3460 km (2149 miles) long.

Forty-seven Bibles are sold every minute.

The Earth travels around the sun at about 107,000 km (67,000 miles) per hour.

Summer and winter on Uranus each last 21 Earth years.

One in five children in the world has never been inside a schoolroom.

There are more insects in a 1.6 km (1 mile) square of rural land than there are people on the planet.

The human heart creates enough pressure to squirt blood over 9 m (30 ft).

A dairy cow will give about 200,000 glasses of milk in its lifetime.

One 75-watt bulb gives more light than three 25-watt bulbs.

Twenty thousand men took 22 years to build the Taj Mahal.

The main library at Indiana University sinks over 2.5 cm (1 in) every year. When it was built, engineers failed to take into account the weight of the books that would occupy the building.

The library at Indiana University finally sinks under the weight of the books after C.J. returns his three overdue library books.

INDIANA UNIVERSITY LIBRARY

It was only two pretty light paperbacks and a comic book!

Bolivia has two capital cities.

A Weddell seal can hold its breath underwater for seven hours.

The height of the Eiffel Tower varies by as much as 15 cm (6 in), depending on the temperature.

Mickey Mouse received 800,000 pieces of fan mail in 1933.

Dear Mickey... I love your squeaky voice ..your big black ears...the way you walk across the screen. Will you marry me?

How did that get in there? That's a POWER BILL!

MICKEY MOUSE READS HIS FANMAIL

The blue whale, the largest animal ever, is 30 m (100 ft) long. It weighs as much as 4 large dinosaurs, 23 elephants, 230 cows or 1800 men.

Almost one-quarter of all mammal species on Earth are bats.

It's like one of those terrible B-Grade vampire movies!

Bats make up one quarter of all mammals on Earth...
And Juan finds the cave in Bolivia where they all live.

Lightning is five times hotter than the surface of the sun.

The Earth is 4.5 billion years old.

The search engine Google got its name from the word 'googol', which is the number one with a hundred zeros after it.

It takes nearly 2500 cows to supply the USA's National Football League with enough leather to make a year's supply of footballs.

The leaves of some water lilies can be 2.4 m (8 ft) wide.

In Haiti, only one out of every 200 people owns a car.

Pain travels through the human body at a speed of over 106 m (350 ft) per second.

The sun makes up 99 per cent of the matter in our solar system.

The weight of all the insects on Earth is twelve times greater than the weight of all the people on Earth.

The average person spends three years of their life on the toilet.

A person drinks about 75,000 litres (20,000 gallons) of water in his lifetime.

The human head contains 22 bones.

Lightning strikes the Earth 100 times every second or 6000 times every minute.

One bat can consume 1000 mosquitoes in a single hour.

The average lead pencil can be used to draw a line 56 km (35 miles) long or to write approximately 50,000 English words.

The wingspan of a Boeing 747 is longer than the Wright brothers' first flight.

No piece of dry, square paper can be folded in half more than seven times.

If all the blood vessels in your body were placed end to end, they would make a line about 96,000 km (60,000 miles) long.

In one day your heart beats 100,000 times.

At a steady jogger's pace of 10 km (6 miles) per hour, it would take 173 days to go around the equatorial circumference of Earth, and more than five years to go around Jupiter, the largest planet.

There are more than 3500 living species of cockroaches.

A human's small intestine is 6 m (20 ft) long.

Scientists estimate that there are at least 15 million stars for every person on Earth.

Some kinds of bamboo grow 89 cm (35 in) in one day.

It is estimated that 6800 languages are spoken in the world today.

You blink over ten million times in a year.

The most drought-resistant tree is the boab tree. It can store 163,000 litres (35,800 gallons) of water in its trunk for later use.

CHOP
CHOP
GUSH

It was while chopping firewood in the Outback that Jack discovered the difference between a gumtree and a Boab tree is about 163,000 litres of water.

Three hundred and fifteen entries in Webster's 1996 dictionary were misspelled.

Rats multiply so quickly that in 18 months, two rats could have more than one million descendants.

The combined wealth of the world's 250 richest people is greater than the combined wealth of the poorest 1.5 billion people.

Outer space begins 80 km (50 miles) above the Earth.

The first number plates were introduced in 1893.

Reginald Smith pays big money for the first number plate in 1893 and receives the first speeding ticket soon after.

When awake, cats spend up to 30 per cent of their time grooming.

During a typical human life, a heart will beat approximately 2.5 billion times.

A hippopotamus can open its mouth 1.2 m (4 ft) wide.

An elephant can smell water nearly 5 km (3 miles) away.

Nicaragua had 396 different rulers between 1839 and 1855; their average reign lasted less than 15 days.

Each year chickens lay 400 billion eggs.

A human sneeze exits the mouth at almost 480 km (300 miles) per hour. This is the speed of the wind in a class five tornado.

The fastest moon in our solar system circles Jupiter once every seven hours. It travels faster than 112,000 km (70,000 miles) per hour.

The largest jellyfish ever found was 2.3 m (7.5 ft) long.

Besides inventing the telephone, Alexander Graham Bell set a world water speed record of 113 km (70 miles) per hour in a hydrofoil boat.

There are approximately 31.5 million seconds in a year.

Around ten per cent of all the people who ever lived are alive today.

The moon has no atmosphere, so footprints left there by astronauts should remain for at least ten million years.

On average, 100 people choke to death on ballpoint pens every year.

There are 2,598,960 five-card hands possible in a 52-card deck of cards.

The oldest fish in captivity lived to 88 years of age.

Entertainment and the Arts

When young and poor, Pablo Picasso kept warm by burning his own paintings.

It's my greatest work yet! It's about lots of little stars twinkling brightly in the sky at night over Austria. Something kids can sing along to. I'll call my masterpiece... TWINKLE TWINKLE LITTLE STAR.

After gazing at the night sky for ten minutes Mozart comes up with a great idea.

'Twinkle Twinkle Little Star' was written by Mozart.

Director George Lucas had trouble getting funding for the movie *Star Wars* because most film studios thought people would not go and see it.

Mel Blanc, who was the voice of Bugs Bunny, was allergic to carrots. He had to chew a carrot for a take, then spit it into a bucket.

Leonardo da Vinci spent 12 years painting *Mona Lisa*'s lips.

Walt Disney was afraid of mice.

The most popular movie star in 1925 was the dog Rin Tin Tin.

Spot is mistaken for the famous Rin Tin Tin in the street.

Pinocchio is Italian for 'pine eyes'.

In *Casablanca*, Humphrey Bogart never said 'Play it again, Sam'.

Donald Duck comics were once banned in Finland because Donald does not wear pants.

The Bible has been translated into Klingon.

Boxing is the most popular theme in movies about sport.

Tom Sawyer was the first novel written on a typewriter.

Author Mark Twain gives up the fountain pen and wrestles with new technology.

The world's longest-running play is *The Mousetrap*. It is a murder mystery that was written by Agatha Christie in 1947. It has been performed over 20,000 times.

The first four countries to have television were England, the USA, the USSR and Brazil.

Donald Duck's middle name is Fauntleroy.

'The Muppet Show' was banned in Saudi Arabia because one if its stars was a pig.

Alfred Hitchcock did not have a belly button. It was eliminated when he was sewn up after surgery.

Virginia Woolf wrote all her books standing up.

Before the 1960s, men with long hair were not allowed to enter Disneyland.

The King of Hearts is the only king in a deck of cards with a moustache.

Dad's just gonna love these personalised playing cards!

Nigel found to his surprise that in the deck of cards only the King of Hearts had a moustache. So with a quick flick of the felt pen ...everyone had a moustache ...and eyes...and hair ...lots of hair...all of it black.

Mark Twain, one of America's best-loved authors, dropped out of school when he was 12 years old, after his father died.

In 1938, the creators of Superman sold the rights to the character for $65 each.

During the chariot scene in *Ben Hur* a small red car can be seen in the background.

Vincent Van Gogh only sold one painting in his life and that was to his brother.

The first time a toilet was flushed in a movie was in *Psycho*.

In Finland, Cinderella is known as Tuna.

X-rays of the *Mona Lisa* show that there are three completely different versions, all painted by Leonardo da Vinci, under the final portrait.

The sound effect of ET walking was made by someone squishing jelly in her hands.

Every time Beethoven sat down to write music, he poured cold water over his head.

Leonardo da Vinci could write with one hand and draw with the other at the same time.

The people of Iceland read more books per capita than any other people in the world.

The name of Oz in the *Wizard of Oz* was thought up by the creator, Frank Baum, when he looked at his filing and saw O–Z.

The idea of a countdown before a rocket launch originated as a tension-building device in the 1929 movie *The Woman on the Moon*.

The first film with spoken dialogue premiered on 6 October 1927 in New York. It was *The Jazz Singer* starring Al Jolson.

Many of the details we associate with Santa Claus were invented for a Coca Cola advertising campaign around 1890.

The longest movie runs for 85 hours and is fittingly titled *The Cure for Insomnia*.

Twenty-seven Ludicrous Laws

Illinois: It is illegal to give lighted cigars to dogs, cats or other pets.

Pacific Grove, California: It is a misdemeanour to kill or threaten a butterfly.

Florida: Men may not be seen publicly in any kind of strapless gown.

Sarasota, Florida: It is illegal to wear swimwear while singing in a public place.

Belgium: Every child must learn the harmonica at primary school.

Florida: If an elephant is left tied to a parking meter, the parking fee has to be paid.

Minnesota: It is illegal to mock skunks.

Virginia: All bathtubs must be outside, not in the house.

Somalia, Africa: It is illegal to carry old gum on the tip of your nose.

Toronto, Canada: It is illegal to ride streetcars on Sundays after eating garlic.

Milan, Italy: Citizens can be fined $100 if seen in public without a smile on their face. Exemptions include time spent visiting patients in hospitals or attending funerals.

Alaska: It is illegal to look at or pursue a moose from a flying vehicle.

Turkey: In the sixteenth and seventeenth centuries, anyone caught drinking coffee was put to death.

Oklahoma: People who make ugly faces at dogs may be fined and jailed.

Ancient Egypt: The penalty for killing a cat, even by accident, was death.

Chicago, Illinois: It is illegal for a woman who weighs more than 91 kg (200 lb) to ride a horse while wearing shorts.

Fairbanks, Alaska: It is illegal to give a moose a beer.

San Francisco: It is illegal to use old underwear to clean cars in a car wash.

Russia: During the time of Peter the Great, any man who wore a beard had to pay a special tax.

New York: It is illegal to let your dog sleep in the bathtub.

Florida: It is illegal to doze off under a hairdryer.

Avignon, France: It is illegal for a flying saucer to land in the city.

Paraguay: Duelling is legal as long as both people are registered blood donors.

Switzerland: It was once against the law to slam your car door.

Gunther loses the very same door his wife slammed in an argument only ten minutes before in the fast lane of the motorway at 120 kph.

Athens, Greece: A driver's licence can be taken away if the driver is deemed either unbathed or poorly dressed.

Louisiana: Biting someone with your natural teeth is assault, while biting someone with your false teeth is aggravated assault.

New York: It is illegal to do anything against the law.

Rather than break the law of New York... King Kong decides to climb to the top of the Empire State Building... ...just for a look around this time.

History Never Repeats

The parachute was invented by Leonardo da Vinci in 1515.

Cleopatra was Greek, not Egyptian.

In 1867, the Russian Czar Alexander II sold Alaska for about $7.2 million to the USA to pay off his gambling debts. At the time, most people thought this was a really bad deal for the USA.

In the Middle Ages, pepper was used for bartering, and it was often more valuable than gold.

Early bagpipes were made from the livers of sheep.

Hawaii officially joined the USA on 14 June 1900.

Athletes in the ancient Olympics competed in the nude.

The Japanese throne has been occupied by a member of the same family since the sixth century. The present emperor is the 125th in succession.

The first vending machine was invented in 215 BC and was a water dispenser.

The Roman Empire existed from about 700 BC, when legend has it that Romulus and Remus founded Rome, to 1453, when the Eastern, or Byzantine, branch of the Empire fell to the Turks.

The umbrella originated in ancient Egypt, where it was used by the royal family and nobles as a symbol of rank.

The Vikings reached North America
500 years before the Pilgrims.

The dinosaurs were on Earth for
almost 150 million years. That is
75 times longer than humans have been
on the planet.

Napoleon
Bonaparte
designed
the Italian
flag.

I don't know which one of these
flag designs I like the most! They're
both wonderful!

Napoleon Bonaparte who
fancies himself as a
flag designer... works on
some ideas for the
Italian flag.

Before 1800, separate shoes for right and left feet were not designed.

I don't think these new left and right shoes will catch on. They're too hard to remember which one goes on which foot!

Edward tries out the first pair of left and right shoes in 1800.

Tea is believed to have been discovered in 2737 BC by a Chinese emperor when some tea leaves accidentally blew into a pot of boiling water.

Henry III became king when he was ten months old.

The first email was sent in 1972.

A squirrel closed down the New York stock exchange one day in 1987 when it burrowed through a phone line.

In ancient Egypt, certain baboons were mummified when they died.

The American army tried to train bats to drop bombs during World War II.

Denmark has the oldest existing national flag. The flag dates back to the thirteenth century.

The oldest toy in the world is the doll. It was invented in Greece about 3000 years ago.

In the tenth century, the Grand Vizier of Persia carried his library on 400 trained camels. The camels had to walk in alphabetical order.

The story of Cinderella originated in China.

It was widely believed in the Middle Ages that the heart was the centre of human intelligence.

In ancient Egypt, men and women wore eyeshadow made from crushed beetles.

In the nineteenth century, the British navy attempted to disprove the superstition that Friday is an unlucky day to embark on a ship. The keel of a new ship was laid on a Friday, the ship was named HMS *Friday*, she was commanded by a Captain Friday and she finally went to sea on a Friday. The ship and her crew were never heard of again.

Coca-Cola was originally green.

The oldest existing governing body, the Althing, operates in Iceland. It was established in AD 930.

Leonardo da Vinci invented scissors.

Leonardo Da Vinci quickly invents the scissors to get him out of one of his other inventions ... ..the parachute..

The largest coins were made from copper and were about 1 m (3 ft) long and 60 cm (2 ft) wide. They were used in Alaska in the nineteenth century and were worth $2500.

Democracy began 2500 years ago in Athens, Greece.

The Sumerians, who lived in the Middle East, invented the wheel in about 3450 BC.

Sure it rolls!
It's a bit CLUNKY...
But it rolls...
Anyway... what's a
bump or two?

The ROUND WHEEL was invented
by the Sumerians.
On the other hand...
the not so well known
useless SQUARE WHEEL
was invented by an
unknown tribe... somewhere else.
And never made it into the history books!

Leonardo da Vinci invented an alarm clock that woke you by tickling your feet.

The first toy balloon, made of vulcanised rubber, was invented in London in 1847.

The Olympic torch and flame were invented by Germany for the 1936 Berlin Olympics.

Illegal gambling houses in eighteenth-century England employed a person to swallow the dice if there was a police raid.

The first message sent over Graham Bell's telephone on 10 March 1876 was 'Mr Watson, come here, I want you'.

In the Philippines during the 1500s, the yo-yo was made of stone and used as a weapon.

Ancient Egyptians slept on pillows made of stone.

Napoleon Bonaparte was afraid of cats.

The Battle of Waterloo is called off when Napoleon catches sight of a large ginger tom strolling across the battlefield.

Tomato sauce was sold in the 1830s as medicine.

In *Gulliver's Travels*, Jonathan Swift described the two moons of Mars, giving their exact sizes and speeds of rotation. He did this more than 100 years before the moons were discovered.

The word 'checkmate' in chess comes from the Persian phrase 'Shah Mat', which means 'the king is dead'.

Dentists in medieval Japan extracted teeth by pulling them out with their fingers.

Hitler was *Time* magazine's Man of the Year in 1938.

Cleopatra sometimes wore a fake beard.

Prior to World War II, when guards were posted at the fence, anyone could walk up to the front door of the American president's residence, the White House.

Early Greeks and Romans used dried watermelons for helmets.

The first daily television broadcast began in 1936 on the BBC.

Before the first television broadcast in 1936...and before they had a television in the corner of the room...the Smith family would sit gazing at a bowl of flowers, sipping tea until bedtime.

Karate originated in India, but was developed further in China.

Weird

World

Facts

The Earth spins at 1600 km
(1000 miles) per hour at the equator.

The Earth rotates more slowly on its axis in March than in September.

Europe is the only continent without a desert.

The Pacific Ocean is not as salty as the Atlantic Ocean.

Believe me! When you've been lost at sea for two weeks..and you try drinking it... Every ocean is just as salty as the next bit.

Diamonds are flammable.

The Earth flies through space at more than 100,000 km (66,600 miles) per hour.

The largest continent is Asia.

Micro-organisms can be found as deep as 3.5 km (2 miles) in the Earth's crust.

The South Pole is colder than the North Pole.

The first living creature to orbit the Earth was a dog sent into space by the Russians.

In a study by the University of Chicago in 1907, it was found that yellow is the easiest colour to spot.

The Greek national anthem has 158 verses.

The moon moves 3.82 cm (1.5 in) away from the Earth every year.

Bishop's Rock in the UK is the smallest island in the world.

Damascus in Syria is the oldest inhabited city. It was founded in 753 BC.

In the Amazon rainforest, 2.5 sq km
(1 sq mile) can be home to 3000 species
of trees.

Australia is the only country that takes
up an entire continent.

A storm officially becomes a hurricane when it reaches wind speeds of 119 km (74 miles) per hour.

You know when strong wind becomes a hurricane when the windspeed reaches 119 km per hour.... or... when cows and cars start flying past you.

The British flag should only be called the Union Jack when it is on a ship at sea.

The deepest part of the Pacific Ocean is 11 km (6.8 miles).

There are more than 50,000 earthquakes throughout the world every year.

The centre of the Earth is believed to be as hot as the surface of the sun.

Every year in Sweden a hotel is built out of ice. It melts, then it is rebuilt the next year.

Icebergs have been fitted with sailing gear and sailed 3840 km (2400 miles).

Bigger raindrops make brighter rainbows.

Proportionally speaking, the Earth is smoother than a billiard ball.

The Earth is slightly hotter during a full moon.

Russia and America are less than 4 km (2.5 miles) apart at their closest point.

There are solar-powered pay phones in the Saudi Arabian desert.

An estimated 95 per cent of all forms of life that once existed on Earth are now extinct.

Waves in the Pacific Ocean can be up to 34 m (111 ft) high.

The Earth is 80 times the size of the moon.

It takes eight minutes and 17 seconds for light from the sun to reach Earth.

The Amazon River pushes lots of water into the Atlantic Ocean. In fact, there is fresh water in the ocean more than 160 km (100 miles) from the mouth of the river.

The average meteor is no larger than a grain of sand, but it is moving at nearly 48,000 km (30,000 miles) per hour when it enters the atmosphere. This makes it burn so brightly that it is seen as a 'shooting star' from the ground.

Eighty per cent of people who are hit by lightning are men.

A raindrop falls at about 12 km (7.5 miles) per hour.

Food for Thought

In Vietnam, there is a drink made from lizard blood.

Chewing gum can keep a person from crying while cutting onions.

Fine-grained volcanic ash is an ingredient in some toothpastes.

Black pepper is the most popular spice in the world.

A Tanzanian dish is white ant pie.

Some Amazonian tribes like to barbecue tarantulas and eat them. Apparently they taste like prawns.

Banana plants cannot reproduce themselves. They must be propagated by people.

The blue whale needs to consume 6.3 million kilojoules (1.5 million calories) a day.

Peanuts are one of the ingredients in dynamite.

A Japanese dish is grilled beetle grubs.

Canned food was invented in 1813, but a practical can opener was not invented until 1870.

Koalas do not drink water.

Bubble gum contains rubber.

A favourite dish in Mexico is lamb brain tacos.

The microwave was invented in the 1940s after a researcher walked by a radar tube and discovered that a chocolate bar in his pocket had melted.

Until the sixteenth century, carrots were black, green, red and purple. Then a Dutch horticulturist discovered some mutant yellow seeds that produced an orange colour.

You are more likely to be killed by a champagne cork than by a venomous spider.

Despite a venomous spider being on the loose at the wedding... It was the bride's father with a champagne bottle they really had to fear.

Eating an apple will make you feel more awake in the morning than drinking a cup of coffee.

Most lipsticks contain fish scales.

Wacky Word Facts

No words in the English language rhyme with month, orange, silver or purple.

'Go' is the shortest sentence in the English language.

GO...!

Oh! Is that it? You mean I was waiting all day just to hear that sentence?

The word 'paradise' was once the Persian word for a royal amusement park.

The Cambodian alphabet is the largest. It has 74 letters.

The Hawaiian alphabet consists of only 12 letters.

The longest word in English is 'pneumonoultramicro-scopicsilicovolcanoconiosis'.

Aardvark means 'earth pig'.

The only 15-letter word that can be spelled without repeating a letter is 'uncopyrightable'.

The Inuit have 20 different words for snow.

Dr Seuss invented the word 'nerd'.

'Zorro' is Spanish for 'fox'.

The word 'news' is actually an acronym for the four compass points (<u>n</u>orth, <u>e</u>ast, <u>w</u>est and <u>s</u>outh).

Attics were invented in Attica.

The first word spoken on the moon was 'Okay'.

The oldest word in the English language is 'town'.

The gorilla's scientific name is *Gorilla gorilla*.

The longest one-syllable word in the English language is 'screeched'.

More people in China speak English than in the USA.

The dot over the letter 'i' is called the tittle.

Butterflies used to be called 'flutterbys'.

The 'sixth sick sheik's sixth sheep's sick' is the toughest tongue-twister in the English language.

A 'spat' is a baby oyster.

Newton is the most common place name in Britain. There are 150 places with that name.

'Of' is the only word in which an 'f' is pronounced like a 'v'.

'Bookkeeper' and 'bookkeeping' are the only words in the English language with three consecutive sets of double letters.

The word 'taxi' is spelled the same in English, German, French, Swedish and Portuguese.

The most used letter in the English alphabet is 'e', and 'q' is the least used.

The word 'karaoke' means 'empty orchestra'.

The sentence 'the quick brown fox jumps over the lazy dog' uses every letter in the alphabet.

Strange Science

Glass is made from sand.

Glass, which looks like a solid, is actually a very slow moving liquid.

Velcro was invented by a person who studied the burrs that clung to his dog's coat after a walk.

White light is a mixture of all the colours in the spectrum.

Some forms of primitive life can survive anywhere that water is found, even in boiling water or ice.

The sound of a whip cracking is actually a mini sonic boom that occurs when the tip of the whip breaks the sound barrier.

Eleanor Roosevelt received a telegram from the 1939 World's Fair in New York that used only the power from electric eels.

Using nanotechnology, a microscopic guitar with strings has been made. It is no larger than a blood cell.

During one four-year period, inventor Thomas Edison registered almost 300 patents.

John Logie Baird made the first television in 1924 using cardboard, scrap wood, needles, string and other materials.

More than a thousand new insects are discovered every year.

Geoffrey discovers some of the one thousand or so new insects found every year on the windshield of his car at 100 kph on the motorway.

A cross between a goat and a sheep is called a 'geep'.

Thomas Edison was afraid of the dark.

Sir Isaac Newton invented the cat flap.

English chemist John Walker never patented his invention of matches because he felt such an important tool should be public property.

Honey is sometimes used in antifreeze mixtures and in the centre of golf balls.

The first stethoscope was made in 1816 with a roll of paper.

Cat urine glows under a black light.

Hot water freezes more quickly than cold water.

The Eiffel Tower always leans away from the sun because heat makes the metal expand.

Patent Mania

Patent no. GB2272154 is for a ladder to enable spiders to climb out of a bath. The ladder comprises a thin, flexible strip of latex rubber that follows the inner contours of the bath. A suction pad on the ladder is attached to the top of the bath.

Patent no. GB2060081 is for a horse-powered minibus. The horse walks along a conveyor belt in the middle of the bus. This drives the wheels via a gearbox. A thermometer under the horse's collar is connected to the vehicle instrument panel. The driver can signal to the horse using a handle, which brings a mop into contact with the horse.

Giddy-up Ginger. Go after that carrot and give us a gallop!

Patent no. GB2172200 is for an umbrella for wearing on the head. The support frame is designed not to mess up the wearer's hair.

Patent no. US4233942 is for a device for protecting the ears of a long-haired dog from becoming soiled by food while it is eating. A tube contains each of the dog's ears. The tubes are held away from the dog's mouth and food while it eats.

Patent no. WO9701384 is for a leash for walking an imaginary pet. It has a preformed shape and supports a simulated pet harness and collar. A micro loudspeaker in the collar is connected to an integrated circuit in the handle, to produce a variety of barks and growls.

Patent no. GB1453920 is for rolled-up fire curtains at roof level on a skyscraper. When a fire starts, the curtains are released to cover the building and suffocate the fire.

Patent no. US5971829 is for a motorised ice-cream cone. The cone spins while you lick the ice cream.

Patent no. US2760763 is for an egg beater that beats the egg within its shell.

Patent no. US6637447 is for the 'Beerbrella'. This is a tiny umbrella that clips onto a beer bottle, keeping the sun off the beverage.

Patent no. WO98/21939 is for deer ears. To use, simply place the deer ears on your head and swivel your new ears in the direction you would like to hear.

Patent no. US3150831 is for a birthday cake candle extinguisher.

Patent no. US5713081 is for three-legged pantihose. When there is a run in the stocking, you simply rotate your leg into the spare hose. The damaged hose is then tucked into a pocket in the crotch of the pantihose.

Patent no. US5719656 is for earless eyewear. Stick the self-adhesive magnets on to each side of your head. The eyewear frames contain internal magnets that hold on to the magnets on your temples.

Patent no. US4022227 is for a three way comb-over to cover a bald head. Just let your hair grow long at the sides, then divide it into three sections and comb it over your bald head one section at a time.

Patent no. US4872422 is for a pet petter. This is an electronic device consisting of an eye that spots your pet and signals the electronic motors to activate the petting arm. The arm is tipped with a human-like hand for added realism.

Patent no. USD342712 is for a frame that clamps around your pet's waist and supports a clear plastic tent-like structure that keeps your pet dry in the rain. There are air holes in the tent.

Patent no. US6557994 is for a way to hang eyeglasses on your face. You use body piercing studs. Pierce your eyebrows and hang your glasses from the studs. There is also a design that works with a nose bridge stud.

Patent no. US4825469 is for a fully inflatable motorcycle suit. When the rider falls off the bike, the suit swells with compressed gas until it covers the head, arms, torso and legs, protecting the rider from damage.

Patent no. US3842343 is for mud flaps to keep mud from flying up the back of your shoes.

Patent no. US6704666 is for the 'Speak & Swing', which is a motorised golf club selection system. You simply speak to your golf bag, telling it which club you want, and the club automatically pops up.

Patent no. US6600372 is for the 'Spitting Duck'. This device fits most toilets and, instead of using toilet paper, you lift the duck's bill and a strategically placed nozzle will spray your bottom with the cleaning formula.

Patent no. US5372954 is for the 'Wig Flipper'. A wig is placed on a large spring and attached to a small cap. The wig and spring are then compressed, locked onto the cap and placed on your head. When you push the spring release button the hairpiece will jump into the air.

Patent US5352633 is for the 'Arm Mitten', which the driver of a car wears on one arm. This protects the arm from sunburn when the elbow rests on the window ledge.

Patent no. US6630345 is for the 'Wonder Butt Bra', which lifts, supports and shapes a person's butt, giving it a desirable shape. It is fully adjustable to fit all sizes of butts.

Patent no. US5848443 is for the 'Travel Relief'. This is a padded toilet for use while driving. It even flushes.

Patent US5375340 is for 'Cool Shoes', which are air-conditioned shoes that have a mini-network of heat exchange coils built into the heels. With each step, the wearer activates the compressor chamber, which forces cool air up into the shoe via a rubber bladder in the sole.

Hilarious

Humans

Every person has a unique tongue print.

Your right lung takes in more air than your left lung does.

People photocopying their butts is the cause of 23 per cent of all photocopier malfunctions.

A woman's heart beats faster than a man's.

The inventor of Vaseline ate a spoonful of the stuff every morning.

Albert Einstein never wore socks.

It is impossible to cry in space because of the lack of gravity.

Astronauts get taller when they are in space.

Bill Gates' house was designed using a Macintosh computer.

Only one per cent of bacteria are harmful to humans.

Your eyes use 25 per cent of your brain power.

In Brazil in 1946, a woman gave birth to decaplets (ten children). She had eight girls and two boys.

The average person blinks about
24 times per minute or about
12.5 million times per year.

To be a NASA astronaut, your height
cannot exceed 182 cm (6 ft).

There are four basic tastes the human tongue can detect. Salty and sweet are tasted on the tip of the tongue, bitter is tasted at the base of the tongue, and sour is tasted along the sides of the tongue.

Wedding rings are worn on the fourth finger of the left hand because people used to believe that the vein in this finger goes directly to the heart.

The average human dream lasts two to three seconds.

Twenty-five per cent of your bones are located in your feet.

Albert Einstein's eyes were auctioned in 1994 after being stored in a safety deposit box since his death in 1955.

The numbers of births in India each year exceeds the entire population of Australia (20 million).

The world's human population was only five million in 5000 BC.

If the population of China lined up and you had to walk the length of the line, you would be walking forever because of all the new births.

Every year, 4000 people injure themselves with teapots.

The measurement from your wrist to your elbow is the same measurement as your foot.

Arteries carry blood away from the heart. Veins carry blood towards the heart.

Nearly ten per cent of American households dress their pets in Halloween costumes.

You breathe in and out about 23,000 times a day.

Girls have more taste buds than boys do.

According to a study by the Economic Research Service, 27 per cent of all food produced in Western nations ends up in garbage bins. Yet 1.2 billion people in the world are underfed.

There are only 200 family names in China for a population of well over a billion.

The average height of people in Western nations has increased by 10 cm (4 in) in the last 150 years.

Douglas Bader was born in London in 1910. He flew for the Royal Air Force in World War II but both his legs were amputated after his aeroplane crashed. He became a flight leader and was instrumental in the Battle of Britain. He attained 23 combat victories by the summer of 1941, making him the fifth highest scoring ace in the RAF.

Roy Sullivan of Virginia, USA, has been hit by lightning seven times.

One out of twenty people has an extra rib.

New Zealand was the first country to give women the vote.

The average person has at least seven dreams a night.

The most common name in the world is Mohammed.

A corpse left out in warm weather will be reduced to a skeleton in about nine days.

In 1973, a confectionery salesman was buried in a coffin made of chocolate in accordance with his dying wishes.

Taste buds last about ten days. Of course, your body is making new ones all the time.

In India, people wear masks on the back of their heads when they go outside. This confuses tigers because they like to attack from the rear.

The Beijing Duck Restaurant in China can seat 9000 people.

Colour blindness is ten times more common in men than in women.

Humans spend a third of their lives
sleeping.

Lack of sleep will kill a person faster
than starvation will.

Come on wakey-wakey!
Rise and shine!
Time to get up
for school!

If people are likely to spend
a third of their lives sleeping...
That means I can stay here for
about twenty five years doesn't it?

Robots in Japan pay union dues.

The Mbuti Pygmies are among the shortest people in the world. The average height for a man is 137 cm (4 ft 6 in) tall.

Boanthropy is a disease that makes a person believe he is an ox.

Tibetans and Mongolians put salt in their tea instead of sugar.

Your tongue is the strongest muscle in your body.

A person cannot taste food unless it is mixed with saliva. For example, if salt is placed on a dry tongue, the taste buds will not be able to taste it. As soon as a drop of saliva is added and the salt is dissolved, the person tastes the salt.

I'm trying to see if I can taste chocolates on a dry tongue.

Trouble is ... My mouth keeps watering! But I'll keep trying anyway!

Mosquitoes are more attracted
to people who have recently eaten
bananas.

Masai tribesman leave their dead out
for wild animals to eat.

There are villages in Papua New
Guinea that are only a twenty-minute
walk apart, but the villagers speak
different languages.

The Neanderthal's brain was bigger
than your brain is.

A pair of leather shoes can supply enough nourishment for a person for about a week.

The average person is 6.2 mm (0.25 in) taller at night.

The Inuit people use fridges to stop their food from freezing.

These walrus steaks are frozen solid. Be a good boy and pop them in the freezer to thaw out please!

The only part of the human body that has no blood supply is the cornea of the eye. It takes in oxygen directly from the air.

Fingernails live for three to six months. They grow nearly 4 cm (1.5 in) a year.

Midgets and dwarfs usually have normal-size children.

In the USA, deaf people have safer driving records than people who can hear.

A 10 cm (4 in) lock of Beethoven's hair sold at Sotheby's for £4000 in 1994.

Forty per cent of dog and cat owners carry pictures of their pets in their wallets.

Only 55 per cent of Americans know that the sun is a star.

Human skin sheds continually. The outer layer of skin is entirely replaced every 28 days.

When D. H. Lawrence died, his ashes were mixed with cement, then used to make his girlfriend's mantelpiece.

The body of Charlie Chaplin was stolen in 1978 from a Swiss graveyard and held for ransom. The sum demanded was 600,000 francs.

Your sense of smell is about five per cent as strong as a dog's.

The pupil of a human eye will expand as much as 45 per cent when it sees something pleasing.

Men sweat 40 per cent more than women do.

The average person laughs 15 times a day.

The largest cell in the human body is the ovum, the female reproductive cell.

During your life, you will eat an average of 70 insects and ten spiders while sleeping.

The most productive mother gave birth to 69 children.

A baby excretes its own weight in faeces every 60 hours.

Although an extremely rare occurrence, sneezing too hard can fracture a rib.

The average human body contains enough fat to make seven bars of soap.